# ANIMAL MUSICIANS

Text **Pedro Alcalde**

Illustrations **Julio Antonio Blasco**

# GIBBON

The word brachiation describes how gibbons use their arms to swing through the trees.

Gibbons are skinny, tailless and long-armed apes. They live like acrobats in the treetops where they eat, play, sleep and yes, sing! It's not unusual to hear their powerful voices from up to 2 kilometres away.

## Duet at Dawn

Every morning, as the sun rises, each gibbon couple sings a duet. To project their voices through the dense vegetation where they live, gibbons use a similar vocal technique as opera singers. They are the jungle divas!

## Technique

Producing a tone that is both high pitched and loud is no easy task, a technique used by professional singers. The gibbons regulate all the components of their vocal instrument, including mouth and tongue. No other ape has this ability. From a young age, gibbons practice daily with their parents resulting in the mastery of the *bel canto* style (meaning beautiful singing).

Youngsters stay with their parents until they are about 6 years old.

Gibbons all live in families and couples often stay together for life.

N.° 12.

NO.

# GIBBON

MR. & MRS GIBBON — Sunrise duet

## Repertoire

In the duet, the gibbon couple will mix their musical parts producing a unique song.

The males evolve their musical sentences from short and simple to long and complex.

Although sometimes they sing simultaneously, each member of the couple often takes turns after the call and response pattern known in classical music as the antiphon.

## About the production

**Concert title**
Duet at Dawn
(for soprano and tenor)

**Venue**
In the Treetops

**Time**
At sunrise

**Length**
Approximately 1 hour

**Composers**
Mr. and Mrs. Gibbon

# Just the facts

**Size**
44 to 60 centimetres

**Weight**
4 to 8 kilograms

**Lifespan**
Up to 30 years

**Habitat**
Rainforest of Southeast Asia: Burma, Thailand, Malaysia and North Sumatra

**Behaviour**
Gibbons are socially active during the day. A family group covers a territory of between 14 to 40 hectares

**Feeding**
Mainly fruit, leaves, flowers, seeds and roots are part of their diet. They also eat insects, spiders, eggs and even small birds

**Enemies**
Hunting and habitat loss due to deforestation are pushing them towards extinction

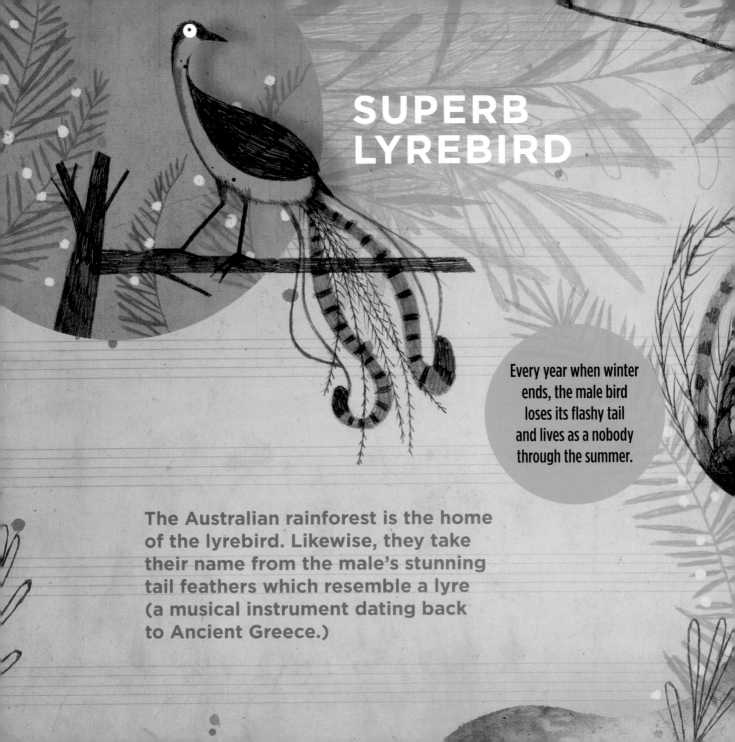

# SUPERB LYREBIRD

Every year when winter ends, the male bird loses its flashy tail and lives as a nobody through the summer.

The Australian rainforest is the home of the lyrebird. Likewise, they take their name from the male's stunning tail feathers which resemble a lyre (a musical instrument dating back to Ancient Greece.)

Possibly the oldest songbird on the planet, the lyrebird is over 15 million years old!

The lyrebird has only three pairs of muscles in the syrinx, instead of the four usually found in songbirds, which gives it a greater flexibility when imitating sounds.

# Rainforest Remix

Many birds can imitate the song of their neighbours, but the lyrebird makes a virtue of this ability. They compose their remixes with the songs of other birds. They may include the sounds of alarms, barking, horns and even the noise of the chainsaw cutting down their own habitat. It is the song of the jungle!

# Technique

After having built a stage in the dense foliage, the male lyrebird gets ready for his show. They can imitate almost any sound they hear for their concerts and dances. Their song is a collage of covers aiming to impress the girl, so an original performance offers a greater chance of attracting a lady friend. Although it might be just for fun, seldom is anybody seen listening!

# SUPERB LYREBIRD

## Repertoire

A lyrebird can imitate over 20 different bird species in a single session by changing their songs into the same tone.

The repetition of some parts of its interpretation ensures the composition's unity.

The courting song of the lyrebird includes not only melodious elements, but many sound effects. And what a wide vocal range: 5 octaves!

## About the production

**Concert title**
Rainforest Remix

**Venue**
Rainforest Disco Club

**Time**
Winter, in courting season

**Length**
About 20 minutes

**Composer**
DJ Lyrebird

# Just the facts

**Size**
80 to 100 centimetres (including a 55 centimetre-long tail)

**Weight**
Approximately 1 kilogram

**Lifespan**
Up to 30 years

**Habitat**
Rainforest of Southeast Australia, and since the 19th century, also in Tasmania

**Behaviour**
They do not stray far from their home

**Feeding**
Creepy crawlies found on the ground such as worms, spiders, cockroaches, larvae, centipedes, small lizards, snails, frogs and on rare occasions, seeds

**Enemies**
Dogs, cats and foxes

# WOLF

Wolves spend 8 hours a day on the move and can cover over 100 km in one night.

Wolves have a scent gland at the tip of their tail, which identifies them with a unique and personal smell.

The wolf is a carnivorous mammal of the same species as the domestic dog. Wolves once lived in great numbers throughout the Northern Hemisphere, but nowadays occupy a much smaller territory.

Howling is an ability taught to wolves at an early age. They receive rewards of caresses and treats when they do their homework well.

Wolf packs have an average of 8 members.

## Twilight Chorus

When evening approaches, just before hunting, a mixed choir of wolves meet with the same level of enthusiasm as a sports team competing in a world championship final. In this atmosphere of camaraderie, the choir sings while listening to their echoes in the mountains. If the hunt succeeds and no injuries occur, the wolves gather again for one last song of celebration.

## Technique

The music begins with one simple note. The remaining members of the choir join in afterwards. During the choral session, each wolf chooses a different note. With their different modulations and rich harmonics, one might think the number of singers is greater than it sounds. Anyone listening to this symphony chorus will be surprised to learn that it's produced by a rather small chamber choir.

# WOLF

The Wolfs

TWILIGHT CHORUS

## Repertoire

The root note of howling has a frequency similar to the human voice and can produce up to 12 harmonics.

Each howl can change notes four or five times. Wolves are masters of the art of glissando, a continuous slide between two notes.

Male wolves produce an 'O' sound, while females produce a more nasal 'U' sound.

One can hear a chorus of wolves over a distance of 10 kilometres in the forest and 16 kilometres across the tundra.

## About the production

**Concert title**
Twilight Chorus

**Length**
1 minute (30-130 seconds)

**Venue**
The Amphitheatre
of the Valley

**Composer**
The Choir of Wolves

**Time**
At dusk (before hunting)

# Just the facts

**Size**
60 to 80 centimetres

**Length**
1,3 to 2 metres long (from muzzle to the tip of the tail)

**Weight**
32 to 70 kilograms

**Lifespan**
8 to 14 years

**Habitat**
A wide variety of ecosystems in the Northern Hemisphere above 30º latitude: forests, mountains, tundra, taiga or prairies

**Behaviour**
They live in organized packs following a strict social hierarchy. A male and female wolf leads each pack

**Feeding**
Sheep, goats, pigs, deer, antelopes, reindeer, horses, moose or bison, and will also eat salmon, rodents or birds

**Enemies**
Humans are their main enemies. Wolves are hunted down because they are a risk to livestock and for sport

# NIGHTINGALE

There is a famous imitation of the call of a nightingale in the second movement of Beethoven's Sixth Symphony. Many composers have dedicated one of their works to the nightingale's song.

The nightingale is a small brown bird with a reddish tail. Towards the end of each April, they sing their passionate songs hidden among the bushes. A symbol of spring and love, nightingales have inspired numerous poems, songs, operas and fairytales around the world.

The song of the nightingale has often been interpreted as a lament although one might consider it joyful instead.

In cities, the nightingale sings even louder and shriller to compensate for the urban background noise.

# Nocturnal Singer

Nightingales sing at night when other birds do not. This adds a curious relevance to their song as they are the only birds heard at those hours. Likewise, they sing with loud, clear notes as if it were an urgent matter.

# Technique

Amongst our feathered friends, the nightingale's song is one of the most complete. Their interpretations resemble a virtuoso holding a wide range of notes, and many shifts in volume and timbre. Included are long and short notes and unique sound effects that go with their birdsong. By originality and ability, the nightingale's stanzas never sound the same granting them a well-deserved reputation. Hence the phrase, he or she sings like a nightingale!

N° 12.

N°.

# NIGHTINGALE

*The Nightingale*
*Singers in the night*

## Repertoire

The nightingale has a vast repertoire making it unique among European songbirds. A bird can produce up to 260 different stanzas in one song.

Various tones make up the stanzas that are both simple and compound.

Sometimes a nearby nightingale may reply in song and continue with another.

Nightingales learn their repertoire during their first year of life.

## About the production

**Concert title**
Nocturnal Singer

**Venue**
The Lowest Branch

**Time**
Between April and June

**Length**
Stanzas lasting 2-4 seconds for hours, until dawn

**Composers**
The Nightingale Troubadour

# Just the facts

**Size**
15-17 centimetres

**Weight**
18-28 grams

**Lifespan**
Can live for 5 years

**Habitat**
In the summer can be found in forests, parks or gardens of Europe and Asia. They spend the winters in tropical Africa. They always return to nest in the same spot

**Behaviour**
They build their nest in mid-May in the bushes nearly touching the ground

**Feeding**
Mainly insects

**Enemies**
Owls, cats, lizards and the pesticides used in farming

# ST. ANDREW'S CROSS SPIDER

When prey lands on her web, she shoots rays of white silk to immobilise her victim before the fatal bite.

After mating, the female attaches her egg sack to the web. The sack contains between 400 and 1,400 eggs.

So named for the pattern in the shape of the St. Andrew's Cross created in the centre of its web. The female spider, whose size outshines the male, does the spinning. Mating is dangerous for the male who is at risk of being devoured by the female as he sets foot on the web. It is vital he offers a good concert since it will affect his chances of survival.

The cross, woven in silk, reflects ultraviolet light, attracting insects.

She hangs upside down with two legs positioned along each arm of the cross.

# Web Serenade

This male spider is a true maestro of the web. Just like a medieval singer, he approaches his dearest to offer her a serenade. The ladies may have poor vision, but make up for this with a superb sensibility for vibrations coming from the web. The suitor's concert must be perfect, or else his musical career could come to a tragic end.

# Technique

The serenade begins with an agitated movement. As the suitor makes the approach, he must play the chords with swiftness. Calmed by the appealing music, the female spider relaxes which reduces the chance of the concert ending before it has begun. As the end nears, our virtuoso spins his own silken thread on the web, and using his six front legs, performs the most intimate musical moments of the evening.

# ST. ANDREW'S CROSS SPIDER

## Repertoire

During courtship, the male spider uses three production techniques: he presses the web, taps it with this abdomen or strums it with his legs.

The female listens using the threads that meet in the centre. They are the tensest and carry the vibrations better.

Spiders do not clap, but if the concert is well received, she will approach and hang from the silk thread spun by the musician.

As with the princess in Puccini's opera, *Turandot*, suitors of this lady risk their lives during courting.

## About the production

**Concert title**
Web Serenade

**Venue**
The Web

**Time**
Summer and autumn

**Length**
Between 10 and 90 minutes

**Composer**
Spider X

# Just the facts

**Size**
3 to 4 millimetres (male) and 10 to 16 millimetres (female)

**Weight**
0.3 to 1 gram

**Lifespan**
1 to 2 years

**Habitat**
East Australia. They live in diverse habitats ranging from tropical forests to city suburbs

**Behaviour**
They spend most of their time in their web. When feeling threatened, they drop from the web or shake it with so much force they manage to confuse their attacker

**Feeding**
Flies, butterflies, moths, bees and beetles

**Enemies**
Preying mantises and birds

# STARLING

During migration they can reach speeds of up to 80 km/hr and cover distances of 1,500 kilometres.

The starling has black plumage with a green or purple shimmer and white spots. Pet starlings can be very affectionate with their owners. When they are not captive, they love flying in a flock creating animated patterns in the sky.

In 1949, so many starlings perched on the hands of London's Big Ben that the clock suddenly stopped.

Mozart wrote in his journal the differences between his score and the starling's song.

## Copying Mozart

A long time ago, on the 27th of May 1784, the famous composer Wolfgang Amadeus Mozart bought a starling as a pet. A short time after writing the music that his bird was singing, it turned out to be one of his own piano concerts! Where did the starling get the melody? It is said Mozart was always whistling. Maybe Mozart himself who, unaware, taught the bird and presto, the starling had learnt the score.

## Technique

It is no easy thing to copy a song. In the first place you need the will to do it; secondly, you require the necessary ability and finally you must pay close attention when listening. Yet starlings do not just copy what they hear. It's true that they may not be the best melody makers in the bird world, but the way they arrange their songs is skillful. They always start with a series of pure tones followed by the central part of the song. From there they continue with changeable parts, which often include fragments of imitated songs. A final singing explosion usually wraps up the session.

# STARLING

"COPYING MOZART"
*Singing Starlight*

## Repertoire

Each starling has its own repertoire including up to 35 different songs and 14 different chatters and warbles.

They have a tendency to sing out of key with unexpected pauses.

It's commonplace for starlings to get distracted and not finish their song. When this happens, they start over.

The birdsong involves a generous number of techniques: whistles, warbles, chatter, rattles, trills and twittering.

## About the production

**Concert title**
Copying Mozart

**Venue**
Anywhere

**Time**
All year round

**Length**
A few minutes

**Composer**
Star Starling

# Just the facts

**Size**
20 centimetres long

**Weight**
60 to 100 grams

**Lifespan**
2 to 3 years

**Habitat**
They make their homes in Europe, North Africa and
Western Asia. But, America and Australia welcomed this
species during the end of the 19th century, and they have
become common there

**Behaviour**
Starlings are migratory birds that fly south in the winter.
They are very sociable and fly in large flocks

**Feeding**
They are omnivores who eat mainly insects,
seeds and fruit

**Enemies**
Hawks, gulls, stoats, racoons and squirrels

# HUMPBACK WHALE

Each humpback whale population has its own migratory route. The longest one goes from Antarctica to the coast of Panama and Colombia.

The humpback whale is one of the largest cetaceans in the world. It has a black back, a protruding head and huge fins that can be over 5 metres long. This ocean giant is not a fish, but rather a mammal and needs to surface above water to breathe.

The females also vocalize but do not take part in the songs.

Often, they include percussion by slapping the water with their fins.

Whales always sing their songs while swimming face-down.

# Singing in the Ocean

In 1955, at the height of the Cold War, installed near the Bermuda Islands were ultra-secret marine microphones recording the movements of Russian submarines. The recording produced many hours of the strangest sounds: the songs of male humpback whales. Fifteen years later, a commercial record of whale songs was released that has since sold over 30 million copies. That's what you call a bestselling album!

# Technique

Humpback whales produce their sound by forcing air through the enormous conducts and cavities of their respiratory system. When they sing, they do not release air. But, they can hold their breath for up to thirty minutes.

Varied sounds are the building blocks for songs. Humpback whales use fixed and sliding notes in all the high and low registers. They also grunt, make sounds through their paired blowholes and may produce pulsed tones to add a little rhythm.

# HUMPBACK WHALE

NATIONAL
GEOGRAPHIC
JANUARY 1979 PAGE 24A

SONGS OF THE
HUMPBACK
WHALE

SIDE 1
33⅓ RPM
STEREO

COMMENTARY BY
ROGER PAYNE, Ph.D.
RESEARCH ZOOLOGIST
NEW YORK ZOOLOGICAL
SOCIETY

MFD. BY EVA-TONE

© 1978 NATIONAL GEOGRAPHIC SOCIETY

## Repertoire

Humpback whale songs are of a complex formation with phrases, themes, rhymes and variations.

Each population of humpback whales sings the same song, changing it slowly over time.

Every song includes various themes arranged in order and lasts between 10 and 30 minutes.

In a singing session, the whale repeats the same song throughout the day which may be why these mammals give the longest concerts in the animal kingdom.

## About the production

**Concert title**
Singing in the Ocean

**Length**
Can last up to 24 hours

**Venue**
The Ocean

**Composers**
The Humpbacks

**Time**
All year round

# Just the facts

**Size**
Males 5 to 17 metres; females 7 to 18 metres

**Weight**
Up to 40,000 kilograms

**Lifespan**
50 years

**Habitat**
The oceans of the world. They are separated into
14 populations according to geographic location

**Behaviour**
They travel the oceans and can cover distances of up
to 25,000 kilometres/year. The population living in the
Persian Gulf is not migratory. They love to jump and leap
out of the water

**Feeding**
Krill, plankton and small fish. Can ingest up to
2,000 kilograms/day

**Enemies**
Humans and orcas

# NORTHERN CARDINAL

When anxious, cardinals raise their feathers on their crest.

The northern cardinal is a radiant songbird. As if its brilliant colour were not enough, the male sports a red coat with black plumage covering its face while an amusing crest clothes its head. Its presence brightens the cold winters where they live, and their endearing song announces the coming spring.

The colour of their plumage comes from the pigments in their food.

The red cardinal is one of the few bird species in the United States where the female also sings.

# Harder Than It Looks

As with other songbirds, the cardinal's song sounds gentle and pure. And yet, how they produce sound is complex.

# Technique

The syrinx is the vocal organ of birds. It divides in two at the lungs, so the songbird has two musical instruments instead of one. What sounds like a single captivating sound is a mixture of two. The cardinal needs perfect control changing from the left side of the syrinx to the right side to interpret their songs. This change may happen up to 16 times per second.

# NORTHERN CARDINAL

Harder than it looks
The Cardinal

## Repertoire

The song starts with a group of ascending sounds, followed by shorter descending ones.

Some of their vocal slides give the impression that northern cardinals have more tones than a piano.

It is the male who teaches the chicks, male and female, how to sing.

## About the production

**Concert title**
Harder Than It Looks

**Venue**
On the Branch

**Time**
All year round, but especially in spring and summer

**Length**
Various sequences lasting 2 or 3 seconds

**Composer**
Sir Cardinal

# Just the facts

**Size**
21 to 23 centimetres

**Weight**
45 grams

**Life span**
Up to 15 years

**Habitat**
Woods, gardens and swamps of Central
and North America

**Behaviour**
They are territorial birds. They are renowned for attacking
their own reflection in windows or mirrors

**Feeding**
Mainly seeds, although they will also eat insects or fruit

**Enemies**
Birds of prey, squirrels, snakes and domestic cats

# CICADA

The nymph lives underground between 2 and 17 years according to the species.

The cicada is an insect with several thousand species scattered around the world. They have small antennae and compound eyes. They are poor jumpers, but their two pairs of transparent, membranous wings make for smooth movement.

When various cicadas perform at the same time in a single concert, they do not go unnoticed!

## Summer Hit

Half of the male cicada's body is like a drum. One could say that he is always crazy in love and that is why he plays his tymbal with high tenacity and energy. His musical activity increases during the warmest hours of the day. Summers would not be the same without cicada concerts.

## Technique

Unlike crickets or grasshoppers, cicadas do not rub their wings, or their legs against a wing, instead they create a vibration in membranes found on both sides of their abdomen. Each syllable of the verse is a back-and-forth movement of the tymbal membrane. The male abdomen is all but empty and works like a soundbox as if it were the chamber of a flamenco guitar.

N. 12.

NO.

# CICADA

SUMMER
HEAT

cicada hit

## Repertoire

The cicada adjusts the sound by pointing its tymbals in different directions.

To recognize its own species, cicadas use distinct ways of combining the drumming of the tymbal.

On creating the sound, the musician shuts his hearing to avoid damage.

As his future partner draws near, the music becomes softer.

## About the production

**Concert title**
Summer Hit

**Length**
Indefinite

**Venue**
The Tree Grove

**Composer**
Cicada Guy

**Time**
In the heat of the day

# Just the facts

**Size**
Between 15 - 65 millimetres in length

**Weight**
25 grams

**Life span**
Between 2 and 17 years as a nymph, depending on the species, and one summer as an adult

**Habitat**
Adults live in trees in temperate and tropical climates

**Behaviour**
Following a long period as a nymph, they shed their skin and become adults with wings

**Feeding**
Tree sap and plants

**Enemies**
Birds, squirrels, bats, spiders or Chinese Shandong cuisine that fries and serves the cicada as a delicacy

# ATLANTIC CANARY

Their fast trill resembles that of a goldfinch who are from the same family.

The Atlantic canary forms a stable couple. Both share domestic duties and the education of their young.

The Atlantic canary is a small, yellowish green bird with chestnut-coloured lines on its back and wings. It takes its name from the Canary Islands and lives throughout Macaronesia.

Their great singing ability goes alongside their exceptional hearing and an excellent memory.

La Serinette was a music box used to teach tunes to canaries.

# The Beauty of Freedom

Perhaps because of its talent as a singer, the Atlantic canary was one of the first birds to be sold as a pet. Since then, 400 years have passed, and the domesticated canary has evolved into a separate subspecies. Even though the domesticated canary has been home-schooled and received constant care, its song has never matched the beauty of the canary's song in the wild. The Atlantic canary's surroundings, with humid laurel forests, softens the metallic ring of its tone making it the most suitable concert hall for its songs.

# Technique

Birds and humans share the ability to learn how to sing. More so with the canary: an apprentice with a fantastic learning capacity. First lessons come from its parents with daily practicing throughout the first year of life. When a canary succeeds in reproducing every aspect of its song, then the song is considered complete.

# ATLANTIC CANARY

## Repertoire

Through perfect synchronization of both sides of the syrinx, they can produce fast and loud trills.

They can master up to 400 different elements, in 30 or 40 songs.

Their song evolves each year as some elements will always change.

Sometimes they even learn the song from their neighbours.

## About the production

**Concert title**
The Beauty of Freedom

**Venue**
Laurel forests

**Time**
All year round

**Length**
More or less 25 seconds per session

**Composer**
Wildbird Canary

# Just the facts

**Size**
10 to 12 centimetres

**Weight**
15 to 20 grams

**Lifespan**
5 to 10 years

**Habitat**
Forests of Canary Islands, Azores and Madeira

**Behaviour**
Make their nests in bushes and trees. They are
non-migratory birds and are social when out of mating
season. Often fly accompanied by over 100 mates

**Feeding**
Seeds, fruit and small insects

**Enemies**
Birds of prey, cats and pesticides

# SAC-WINGED BAT

The sacks in the wings of male bats give off different smells: pleasant to attract the ladies and unpleasant to mark their territory.

The sac-winged bat is black with two white lines going down its back. Although they have wings and fly, bats are not birds but mammals. In fact, they are the only mammals that fly!

The human ear cannot perceive high-pitched ultrasonic sounds.

They will only sing if their loved one is listening and hanging upside-down. They accompany their song with a dance of wings and perfumes.

# Ultrasonic Love Songs

In 1912, after the Titanic ship hit an iceberg and sank, scientists set to solving the problem of avoiding maritime disasters. They studied night-time flying of bats and copied their navigation resulting in the birth of sonar. This technique involved sending out ultrasonic sound waves and receiving a return echo. Interesting fact: bats also use ultrasonic sounds to whisper love songs!

## Technique

Late at night when the sac-winged bats return home, they sing an ultrasonic serenade in the ear of their loved one. They use a vocal repertoire different to the one used for navigation. Instead of short ultrasonic pings, romantic vocalizations include trills, fixed modulated tones, clicks and other sounds. They organize these motives into phrases, and phrases into songs.

# SAC-WINGED BAT

## Repertoire

Trills in different tones are exclusive to the love serenade and are rich in harmonics.

Most of the frequencies of their songs are soundless to the human ear.

Unlike their other vocalizations, they sing serenades at a low volume.

## About the production

**Concert title**
Ultrasonic Love Songs

**Length**
Up to 1 hour

**Venue**
The Private Lounge

**Composer**
Bat Amour

**Time**
At night, upon returning home

# Just the facts

**Size**
5 to 7 centimetres

**Weight**
6 to 9 grams

**Lifespan**
6 years

**Habitat**
The tropical forests of Central and South America

**Behaviour**
They have nocturnal habits. During the day they take refuge in hollow tree trunks. Males do not change harem, but the females do

**Feeding**
Insects caught in full flight

**Enemies**
Birds of prey, more so owls and also snakes, and traps laid by humans

# MUSICIAN WREN

In 1917, the Brazilian composer Heitor Villa-Lobos wrote a marvellous symphonic poem for a large orchestra, in homage to musician wrens.

They only sing when they build their nest in mid-September.

The vast Amazon River region is full of legends about this bird. Their musicality has no equal. They are as shrewd as they are cautious; so one hears them more so than sees them.

Their songs are so melodious that other birds fall silent to hear.

It is said the song of musician wrens brings good luck to whoever hears it.

## Perfect Pitch

If one organized a competition among the creatures of the animal kingdom to discover which is the best at singing in tune, without a doubt the musician wren would be the winner. When it comes to hitting the right notes, they are the best.

## Technique

The musician wren composes songs with pure sounds and a fluted, mysterious tone. It produces the notes without too many harmonic tones nor any other detail that may prove a distraction. Its focus is on the notes and the motives created with them. It only sings for one week each year, and when the brief concert period is over, it twitters, and its qualities as a musician go unnoticed.

# MUSICIAN WREN

UAIRAPURU

*perfect pitch beauty*

## Repertoire

This species always compose their melody with consonant intervals.

Octaves, fifths and fourths are their favorite musical intervals.

Certain pieces by Johann Sebastian Bach begin with motives found in the song of musician wrens.

## About the production

**Concert title**
Perfect Pitch

**Venue**
The Great Amazon Theatre

**Time**
9-12 days a year

**Length**
7-10 minutes

**Composer**
El Maestro Musician Wren, the one and only

# Just the facts

**Size**
11 to 13 centimetres

**Weight**
18 to 24 grams

**Lifespan**
Unknown

**Habitat**
The Amazon rainforest

**Behaviour**
They tend to flutter among the branches of the forest
in the company of their partners

**Feeding**
Mainly invertebrates and occasionally some kinds of fruit.
They tend to seek out ant nests

**Enemies**:
Their main threat is the complete destruction of their
habitat due to logging

# CHINESE TORRENT FROG

They are the only non-mammalian vertebrates that can produce ultrasonic sounds.

Chinese torrent frogs live in the breathtaking Huangshan Mountains in the Chinese province of Anhui. They are light brown with two black lines running down their back. They would not differ from common frogs were it not for their special singing abilities.

The male's head allows for submerged eardrums. This is very infrequent in frogs. Their name in Chinese describes this trait.

Males have two vocal sacks under their mouth that work as powerful amplifiers.

Frogs vocalize with the larynx and vocal cords, just like mammals do.

## Outstanding Music

Frog and toad choirs have something in common: they never sing together. It makes it easier to separate their own voice from another. But the Chinese torrent frogs have another challenge: their natural habitat of torrents and waterfalls is very noisy. To stand out, they created an impressive range of musical solutions making them leaders among their amphibian peers.

## Technique

As the sound of a torrent prevails in low frequencies, Chinese torrent frogs always sing in high frequencies. Their repertoire of songs is infinite. In two full hours of song, they are not likely to repeat the same sounds. With the ability of a songbird or a humpback whale, they change their notes, and they can add or remove sound elements from their notes at will. They really are vocal acrobats!

# CHINESE TORRENT FROG

Chinese
torrent frog

OUT-STANDING SONGS

## Repertoire

Note changing often happens, with multiple rises and falls.

The Chinese torrent frog, without warning, can add or remove harmonic sounds from musical notes.

They are experts in ultrasonic vibrations as they never produce two similar tones.

## About the production

**Concert title**
Outstanding Music

**Venue**
Nine Dragons Waterfall

**Time**
All year round

**Length**
From sundown to midnight

**Composer**
The Torrent Frog

# Just the facts

**Size**
From 3 centimetres (males) to 6 centimetres (females)

**Weight**
12 to16 grams

**Lifespan**
5-8 years

**Habitat**
The dense vegetation surrounding torrents and waterfalls
in Central and Eastern China

**Behaviour**
They take refuge among the humid rocks during the day,
and they live around the torrents at night

**Feeding**
Both aquatic and land invertebrates

**Enemies**
Their main threat is the shrinking of its habitat due to
deforestation and agricultural activities

The feather movement of club-winged manakins is the fastest among vertebrate animals.

# CLUB-WINGED MANAKIN

At first glance, club-winged manakins may appear as ordinary birds. But, if one watches them when they are flirting, it's obvious they have peculiar singing abilities. This is because they sing with their wings, no more, no less.

During courting, they can change branches every second.

Apart from their songs, they include many acrobatic acts in their seduction rituals.

## Musical Wings

Creating sounds akin to a violin is natural for many interpreters in the animal kingdom. This is true of the cricket and lobster. Yet of the existing 10,000 bird species, only the club-winged manakin produces songs in this way.

## Technique

Each of the wings of the club-winged manakin has a feather, with seven crests along the central vein. Alongside this strange feather there is another with a rigid and twisted tip. When manakins raise their wings above their backs, they rub one wing against another with the technique and speed of a great virtuoso.

# CLUB-WINGED MANAKIN

## Repertoire

Each time the twisted feather rubs over a crest from the other feather, it produces a sound. As it has seven crests, when a back-and-forth movement occurs, it creates 14 sounds.

Moving their wings 107 times per second, their mini violin produces 1,498 sounds. You won't even find that in a music conservatory!

To increase resistance, the central vein used as a musical instrument is not hollow inside, as with the other feathers.

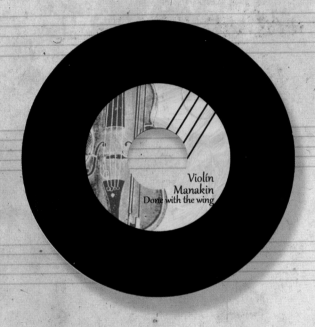

Violín
Manakin
Done with the wing

## About the production

**Concert title**
Musical Wings

**Venue**
The Andean Forest

**Time**
Every day of the year, unless it is changing feathers.

**Length**
Indefinite, its intensity depends on the interest of the audience.

**Composer**
Master Club-Winged Manakin, violin virtuoso

# Just the facts

**Size**
10-14 centimetres

**Weight**
12 grams

**Lifespan**
There are no records

**Habitat**
The Northwestern Andean montane forests
of Colombia and Ecuador

**Behaviour**
They live in the branches of trees

**Feeding**
Insects and small fruits

**Enemies**
Unknown. They appear to live a quiet life